Rivers
and
Lakes

A PENGUIN COMPANY
LONDON, NEW YORK, MUNICH,
MELBOURNE, and DELHI

Written and edited by Simon Holland
and Anna Lofthouse
Designed by Tory Gordon-Harris,
Mary Sandberg, and Venice Shone

Managing editor Sue Leonard
Managing art editor Cathy Chesson
Category publisher Mary Ling
Jacket design Chris Drew
Picture researcher Sean Hunter
Production Shivani Pandey
DTP designer Almudena Díaz
Consultant David Glover

First published in Great Britain in 2003 by
Dorling Kindersley Limited
80 Strand, London WC2R 0RL

2 4 6 8 10 9 7 5 3

ISBN 0-7513-3946-6

Colour reproduction by Colourscan, Singapore
Printed and bound in Italy by L.E.G.O.

European
perch

see our complete
catalogue at
www.dk.com

Contents

Water ways

The world's fresh water is constantly on the move. It flows in and out of lakes, roars down rapids, and runs in rivers to the sea. Its journey never ends.

Water that falls as rain, snow, or hail is not salty. This is why it is known as fresh water.

Great big bathtubs

A lake is a large collection of water that is enclosed by land on all sides. Water from rainfall or melting snow and ice makes its way both overland and underground to fill the lake.

Winding water-chutes

Rivers gather water in much the same way as lakes – but they always have a "source", on high ground, where the flow of water starts.

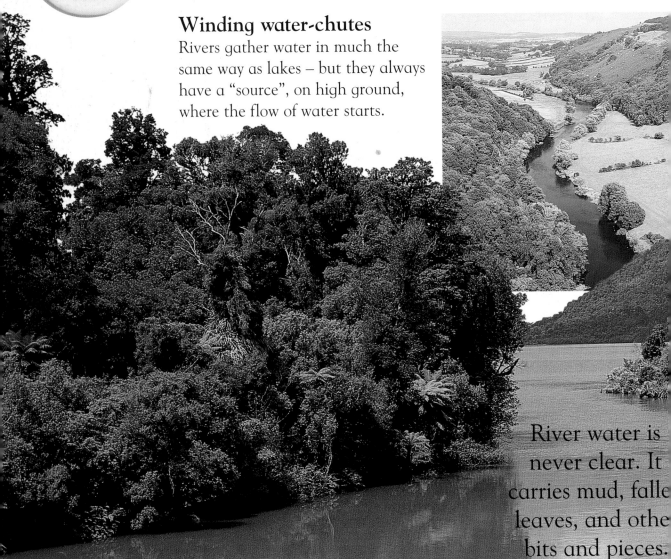

River water is never clear. It carries mud, falle leaves, and othe bits and pieces.

All plants need water to live, grow, and make food for themselves. The banks of rivers and lakes are often teeming with plant and animal life.

THE WATER CYCLE

3

4

1. Water from the oceans and the ground heats up and rises into the air as vapour. **2**. Winds carry the warm, damp air up over higher ground. **3**. The water vapour cools and forms clouds. **4**. Eventually, raindrops form inside the clouds. Then the water falls back down as rain, hail, or snow. **5**. This water makes its way into streams and rivers, either directly, over land, or through the ground. **6**. Rivers then carry the water back into the ocean, and the cycle begins again.

5

1

6

Earth's great artist

...low of water over land slowly ...s away the rocks and moves ...pieces about. Over time, vast ...anyons and dramatic valleys have ...been carved out by moving water.

Source to sea

Rivers have many different stages. Often, they begin as a small spring – an outflow of water from the ground – in a high place. As ground waters and rainwaters add to the source, it becomes a stream.

1. Stream-building

Once the source has grown into a stream, one or more streams, or tributaries, may join with it to form a larger, faster-flowing stream.

2. A young river

As more and more tributaries join the main stream, it will soon become a river with a larger "discharge". This means that the speed and amount of water are building up. As the river moves through steeper land, the speed of the flow becomes greater still, resulting in a stage known as "white-water rapids".

River rapids provide ideal conditions for outdoor water sports such as white-water rafting and canoeing.

. Getting wider

Continuing its journey towards the coast, [the] river then moves into flatter areas of land. [H]ere, the river slows down – but it becomes [w]ider and deeper, suitable for boats and [e]ven large ships.

At this stage, a river will often wind its way through many towns and cities on its way towards the sea.

4. Entering the ocean

Finally, the river approaches its opening into the sea – the estuary, or river "mouth". At this stage it is very broad, and stops looking like a single river. It may split into several smaller, shallow channels cutting through an area of muddy or sandy banks along the coastline.

Black-crowned night herons nest near to river and estuary waters.

Frozen solid

Most of the world's fresh water is stored in its frozen form, as ice and snow, in the Earth's polar regions. In cold climates, where the snow never melts, "rivers" of ice called glaciers are formed.

Frozen falls

In biting cold weather, waterfalls can freeze solid. The thunderous noise of falling water turns to an eerie silence. Only the "scrunch" of ice picks and spiked boots can be heard, as intrepid climbers scale the frozen water.

Water thoughts

● An "ice jam" can occur when a frozen river thaws out. Large bits of ice clog up the flow, which causes flooding.

● Glaciers often produce "roaring" sounds that come out of holes called moulins.

White snakes

In places such as northern USA and Canada, the temperature drops so low in winter that rivers freeze solid. This river is in Alaska. Some remain frozen well into the summer months.

Ice diving

Ice diving is practised by professional divers, who can make money by rescuing trucks and snowmobiles that have been trapped in frozen lakes. It is also becoming a popular new sport.

About 10 per cent of the Earth's land is always covered in ice.

Glaciers store about 75 per cent of the world's fresh water (in the form of ice).

How a glacier forms

Glaciers often occur in mountainous regions, where a lot of snow falls. Fresh layers of snow push down on the older layers beneath, turning them to ice. Over many years, these thick layers of ice form an ice cap. The weight of this ice causes it to creep, slowly, downhill.

Lonely lumps

As they move downhill, glaciers carry rocky material with them. Huge rocks, known as erratic boulders, often become completely stranded as a result.

9

Some river creatures have adapted to the challenge of fast-flowing streams or mountain torrents. Sleek bodies prevent them from being swept away or hurled against the rocks by the current.

Deliberately heavy

Just as human divers put weights on to keep them down in the water, caddisfly larvae give themselves extra weight by producing a glue to stick shells, sand grains, or small pieces of stone to their bodies.

Sleek swimmer

The duck-billed platypus has a streamlined body covered in dense, waterproof fur. Its webbed front feet create a bigger "push" against the water, helping this animal to swim faster.

Clever crayfish

Some creatures stay near the bottom of rivers and let the water flow over their backs. Crayfish have smooth shells and sleek bodies that help to resist the current.

The outer shell of a crayfish is hard. Calcium in the water helps to strengthen the shell.

Trout are at home in cold, bubbly, fast-flowing streams. The bubbles contain a gas called oxygen, which living creatures need to breathe. With this extra oxygen around, the trout can breathe more easily – and so will have enough energy to fight the current.

slope, the faster and stronger the water flow.

Water thoughts

● The Atrato River in Colombia, South America, is the world's fastest-flowing river.

● Trout are part of the salmon family. The species (types) found in rivers and lakes include brook, rainbow, and brown trout.

● The marine (sea) lobster is a relative of the freshwater crayfish.

Room for more inside!

In spring, a male stickleback's throat and underside turn bright red. This is because he has finished making a nest on the bottom of the river, and wants to attract females to lay their eggs inside it.

Adult sticklebacks only have this reddish tinge to their head and belly when they are breeding (producing young).

Home-makers

Whether it is a nest, a den, or a lodge, river creatures are clever at using plant materials to build their homes – either by the riverbank or in the water.

Builder beavers

Beavers use their jaw muscles and sharp teeth to cut down small trees. Gripping on to the materials, they swim to the construction site to build a sturdy home.

Getting cosy

Minks make dens in riverbank holes, tree hollows, beneath logs, or under tree roots. And just as people snuggle inside their homes during cold weather, minks sleep all day in their dens – especially after snow has fallen.

House-proud

The male stickleback has to build and look after his nest on his own. The nest has an opening at each end and a soft, hollow bit underneath for storing his eggs.

A stickleback father may clean the eggs using his mouth.

Male sticklebacks fan fresh water over the eggs in the nest using their fins. This ensures that the eggs have enough oxygen.

Cascade

A river falling over a cliff forms a waterfall. Gentle drops over rocky steps are cascades, while larger amounts of water are cataracts. The noise and spray of plunging rivers create amazing natural wonders of the world.

Awesome Angel Falls

In 1933, James Angel found a waterfall in Venezuela – the highest in the world. It is two and a half times taller than the Empire State Building in New York City, USA.

Widest water veil

On the border of Zimbabwe and Zambia, in southern Africa, the Zambezi River flows to the brink of a dramatic gorge. Here, it crashes down to create the widest sheet of falling water in the world.

Plucky ducks

Torrent ducks are quite fearless. They stand at the bottom of small waterfalls to feed. They like to eat stonefly larvae.

These torrent ducks, from the Andes mountains in South America, spend their whole life in fast-flowing mountain streams.

Watery stairs

Watching waterfalls is
fascinating, as the direct
of the stream turns one wa
and then the other. This Iris
cascade eventually falls into
the Lakes of Killarney.

A rock pool

Feeding frenzy

We humans often eat with a knife and fork, but many river creatures have much more inventive ways of feeding. Some dig, some grab – while others spit or even stab!

"Gotcha!"

Caught! Herons have good eyesight, which they use to scan the water for any signs of life. If a fish comes within striking range, the heron leans forward – partly extending its neck – and then suddenly lashes out with its bill to stab the prey.

Picnickers

Water voles often take their food to places near the water's edge to eat. They like to feed on tasty green leaves and sometimes leave chewed stems behind.

Frog arrest

A giant water bug is able to capture large creatures using its clawed front feet. It can also inject chemicals into the prey. This poison turns the prey's insides into liquid, which the water bug can then suck up as food.

Water arrows

Archerfish are famous for spitting jets of
water at insects above the water. This causes the
insects to drop into the water, where they become
a tasty snack. If an archerfish is very hungry,
it can leap out of the water to catch a fat fly.

*This archerfish
is shooting a fine
stream of water
droplets from
its mouth.*

Dippers and divers

Many creatures live both in and out of fresh water, and some – such as the spectacular kingfisher – have developed eye-catching ways of entering the water. Others are always dipping their heads under the surface to see what is on the menu.

Silvery minnow fish

The kingfisher never uses its bill to spear prey. Instead, it grabs the fish and kills them out of water.

Plunge diver

A quick flash of brilliant blue – that is the sight of a kingfisher diving for any small fish it can grab with its sharp bill. Before diving, a kingfisher hovers over the water, or watches from a branch, ready to strike.

Olympic legs

Most types of frog have long back legs that enable them to take long leaps. They also have webbed feet, which push against the water like a diver's flippers. This means they are good swimmers, as well as impressive jumpers.

BREATHING SPACE

Unlike human divers, the great diving beetle has no need to use any scuba-diving equipment for breathing underwater. Diving beetles can gather together a supply of air by trapping it under their wings, while they are at the surface, before taking it down into the water with them.

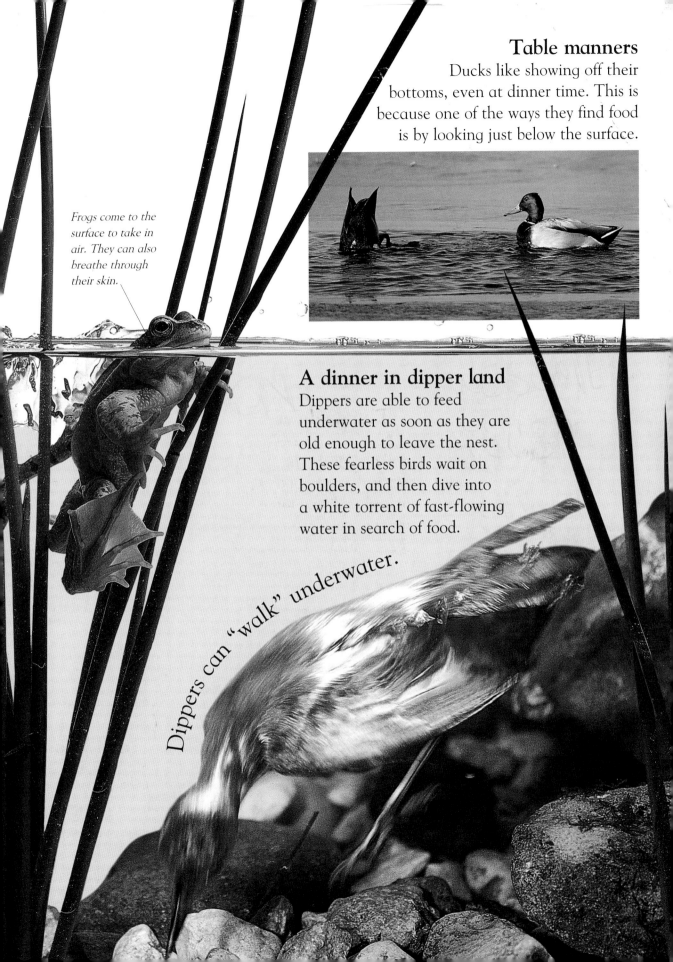

Table manners

Ducks like showing off their bottoms, even at dinner time. This is because one of the ways they find food is by looking just below the surface.

Frogs come to the surface to take in air. They can also breathe through their skin.

A dinner in dipper land

Dippers are able to feed underwater as soon as they are old enough to leave the nest. These fearless birds wait on boulders, and then dive into a white torrent of fast-flowing water in search of food.

Dippers can "walk" underwater.

Wiggly rivers

All rivers "meander", which means that they swing from side to side. Rivers only flow in a straight line if people have built concrete banks on either side.

The river changes direction but remains at a similar width.

A river snake

The river twists and turns, forming a snake-like shape, as it reaches flatter land – the middle part of its journey. The water flows fastest around the outside of the bend, and slower on the inside.

Faster-flowing water travels around the outside of a meander (river bend).

Beaches are formed on the inside bank of some meanders as the water slows down and drops its load of silt and mud.

x-bow lakes

n ox-bow is formed when
meander gets bigger and
gger, creating a narrow-
cked loop. Due to flooding
d erosion, the ox-bow loop
n get cut off completely and
t as a separate lake by the
e of the river.

*Small but deadly – these
red piranha fish, found in
South American rivers,
have razor-sharp teeth.*

V-shaped valleys

Some hill valleys overlap
each other, forming a
criss-cross pattern. This
means that a river has
to bend and twist in
and around the curves
of the land.

Bankside living

Tapirs, crocodiles, and
capybaras all like being near
to tropical rivers. Each animal
has its sense organs (eyes,
ears, and nose) high on its
head so that it can keep out
of trouble when swimming.

Big river dwellers

Although they are not as wide or as deep as the oceans, rivers are home to some big animals. These river creatures have specially adapted bodies for life in the water, such as webbed feet and waterproof fur.

Otter Olympics

Sleek and streamlined – river otters like to play chasing and diving games in the water. Their outer coats are waterproof, and their long, muscular tails help them to swim.

Otters close their nostrils and ears when swimming, to stop the water getting in.

A river rodent

The coypu is one of the world's largest rodents. Its short, rounded ears and small eyes – set high on its head – are used to sense any dangers when in water. Coypu families live in bankside tunnels.

Hefty hippos

Hippos weigh up to 4,500 kg (10,000 lb). With a bulky body and short legs, hippos can move surprisingly gracefully when swimming, walking underwater, or trotting on land. They graze on grass at night and laze in the water during the day.

With its nostrils high on its head, the hippo can keep most of its body underwater and still breathe.

Bloated floaters

West Indian manatees munch their way through lots and lots of water plants. They can stay afloat with ease, even though they are enormous mammals. As they digest the plants they produce lots of gas, which adds to their buoyancy (ability to float).

A manatee uses its flippers for swimming and for pushing food into its mouth.

Water thoughts

● Manatees can remain under the water for up to 20 minutes before rising to the surface to breathe.

● Hippos search for food on land at night and have been known to eat sugarcane and corn.

● Otter cubs learn to swim just three months after they are born.

About lakes

A lake is a big area of water, enclosed by land. Lakes form when water flows into a hollow or crater faster than it can escape. Melting ice and snow on mountain tops, for example, feed lakes in the valleys below.

Lakes in craters

Exploded volcanoes leave holes, called craters, behind. If the base of an inactive volcano's crater is solid, the water cannot escape. As a result, lots of water collects and a crater lake is formed.

All types...

A crystal-clear lake nestled at the bottom of a mountain looks beautiful, but not all lakes are like this. Earth has a tremendous variety, from small fish ponds to the largest freshwater lake of all – Lake Superior, in North America.

40 per cent of the world's total lake water is in Lake Baikal, Russia

Dragonflies are racing champions that can fly at speeds of up to 95 kmh (60 mph).

The Great Lakes

Superior, Michigan, Huron, Erie, and Ontario, plus their connecting channels, form the largest area of fresh water on the surface of planet Earth. These five enormous lakes are visible from the Moon.

Man-made lakes

A reservoir is a man-made lake, which is formed when a dam is built on a river. The river water backs up behind the dam to create the reservoir.

A water bird called a reed warbler weaves its nest around reed stalks.

Reedmaces have distinctive brown "pokers" full of thousands of seeds.

and the Great Lakes of North America.

Life on a lake

Lake life involves a host of submerged (underwater) plant and animal species, but it is important to remember that there is also a lot going on at the surface.

Built to travel

Water boatmen are talented movers. They use their oar-lik back legs to "row" across the surface of a pond. Thanks to their wings, they can also leap out of the water and fly away.

Alert! Alert!

The highly sensitive eyes and whiskers of this giant otter car detect very tiny movements in the water. This helps the otter to capture the prey on which it feeds, such as fish and crabs.

Giant otters can grow to 1.4 m (4.6 ft) in length, which is about the height of a child.

Plant platforms

Giant water lilies, in the Amazon region of South America, can measure up to 1.2 m (4 ft) across and are strong enough to hold a small child. Floating plants, such as water lilies, benefit from receiving a lot of sunlight, which they use to make their food.

Walking on water

The wattled jacana bird is also known as the "lily-trotter". It has extremely long toes, which spread out its weight so that it can run along floating plants or the surface of the water.

Floating water plants make great homes for birds, molluscs, worms, spiders, and crustaceans.

Giant water hyacinths

Male jacanas build the nest, while the females, which are much bigger, defend it from predators.

Jacanas build their nests on floating vegetation.

27

What lurks in lakes

The deeper parts of a lake, down to the very bottom, receive less and less light. In these darker and murkier waters, creatures can hide away and surpris their prey.

Pike bites

A pike lies in wait, well-hidden, or camouflaged, among brown waterweeds. The pike remains very still, then bursts out to snap up passing fish, or any other meaty meals.

Sideways sensing

This toad has sense organs along its sides. The organs detect tiny vibrations in the water, which help it to find foo and avoid predators in the murky waters at th bottom of lakes and ponds.

African clawed toad

A LURKING LEGEND

As legend has it, a lake in Scotland is home to a creature called the Loch Ness Monster – or "Nessie" for short. People claim to have seen a huge hump, with a long, giraffe-like neck casting a dark shadow on the surface of the lake. Those eager to prove the existence of the monster have used all sorts of technology to try and find it.

uppy power

mudpuppy has a flattened, eel-
ke body so that it can burrow (dig)
nder rocks and logs. It also has
eathery red gills that make it look
ke it is wearing a long red scarf!

Dragonfly nymph

Dragonfly nymphs
hatch out of eggs laid
in water. These young
dragonflies are the
same colour as the
bottom of the pond or
lake. This helps to hide
them from predators.

Nervous newts

Newts are shy creatures
that hide in damp places
or underwater. They have
slimy skin, a long tail, and a
rounded head. Some walk
over the muddy bottoms
of ponds using just the
tips of their fingers and
toes – similar to a
person creeping
about on tiptoe.

These newt
tadpoles are only
a few weeks old.

29

Swampy wetlands

Muddy coastlines, where rivers approach the sea, are sometimes edged with swamps, marshes, and mangrove forests in tropical parts of the world. Salty water washes in and out of these areas as the tides come and go.

Swamp snakes

The poisonous cottonmouth snake lives in swamps, bayous, and slow-moving rivers in southeastern USA. It got this name because of its pure white mouth, which can be seen each time the snake displays its fangs.

Low tide take-away

Fiddler crabs cannot fee underwater. They have wait until low tide, whe they emerge from the burrows to pick sm bits of food fro the mu

Mudskipper fish have strong front fins and a special sucker on their belly, which help them to climb up and cling on.

Fish out of water

As the tide comes in, mudskippe climb up mangrove roots and branches to avoid predator When the tide is out, they plop down onto the mangr floor to feed on creatures living in the mud flats.

The mangrove floor is covered in prop roots, which are easier to see when the tide is out.

A tangled mess

The trees in a mangrove forest have roots that grow into the air instead of down into the soil! These "aerial roots" allow the tree to breathe in the salty water. Meanwhile, "prop roots" hang down into the mud to give the tree extra support.

The mouth

An estuary, or river "mouth", is where the river's freshwater flow finally comes to the end of its journey and runs into the ocean. This part of a river is a mixture of land and sea, and of fresh water and salt water.

Half river, half sea...
River estuaries are affected by the tides of the sea, but are protected from waves, winds, and storms by the surrounding banks of sand, land, and mud.

Chisel-beaks

Oystercatchers feed on mussels, limpets, and cockles. They get into the shells by chopping the muscle that holds the shell halves together, or by bashing them open against rocks or sand.

Search and destroy

Avocets find food in the wet mud. They sweep their long, curved bill to and fro in search of small worms and shrimps.

Pied avocet

Mud flats are as useful to a wading bird as fridges and larders are to human beings.

Mud flats

As a river nears the sea, where the land is flatter, it slows down and dumps its load of mud and sediment. This creates huge areas of mud where flocks of birds come to feed.

THE THINKER

Herons are quite intelligent when it comes to catching fish. The black heron spreads its wings to cast a shadow on the water. This attracts groups of fish, because they like to bask in the shade. The heron then grabs them with a quick thrust of its bill. Like fishermen, some even use bait to lure their catch.

Taking shell-ter

Estuary-dwelling creatures, such as shellfish, find protection from birds and other predators at high tide. For extra safety, some only hunt at night.

Purple crab

Hermit crab

35

Salmon marathon

Travelling is an important part of a salmon's life. Born upstream in rivers, the young salmon migrates (travels a long way) to the ocean to feed and grow. When ready to spawn (lay eggs) it swims thousands of kilometres back to the river where it first hatched.

People fish for the large adult salmon as the fish return to the streams where they were born.

1. To the river

Once they have reached their destination, the female sockeye salmon dig a nest in the gravelly river bed – where they lay up to 4,300 bright pink eggs, which the males then fertilize.

2. To the lake

As soon as the sockeye salmon fry (baby salmon) hatch and emerge from their gravel nest, they make their way towards the nearest lake.

When they set off for the freshwater lake, salmon fry are only about 11 cm (4.3 in) long at the most.

3. To the sea

After spending about a year in a freshwater lake, the sockeye salmon journey to the saltwater ocean, where they will remain for most of their life. At this time, they have blue-grey heads and backs, and silvery sides.

The powerful jaws and paws of

Brown bears try grab the spawni salmon as they le above the surface duri their journey upstrea

34

4. The final lap

About four years into
their life, the adult
salmon return to their
home streams to breed,
sometimes travelling as far
as 1,500 km (930 miles).
After spawning, they die.

the brown bear are a danger to salmon.

Water thoughts

● When the sockeye salmon
leave the ocean, their bodies
turn from silver to bright red.

● A salmon's strength can
be defeated by turbines and
sluiceways in river dams.

● Sockeye salmon live in the
USA, Japan, the Canadian
Arctic, and Siberia.

Stop the flow

People build dams to restrict and control the flow of water in a river. Throughout history, dams have been used to prevent flooding and to irrigate (water) farmland. Today, they are also used to produce electricity.

Giant cork

The Glen Canyon Dam, in Arizona, USA, is 216 m (710 ft) tall and 91 m (300 ft) thick at the bottom. The restriction of the water causes an artificial lake (a reservoir), called Lake Powell, to build up behind the dam

Once the dam was built, it took 17 years for Lake Powell to completely fill up behind the barrier.

This is the Glen Canyon Bridge.

Diversion ahead

Often, a river has to be diverted (moved elsewhere) while a dam is being built. Builders took three years to carve a new channel for the Paraná River, in Brazil and Paraguay, so that they could construct the Itaipú Dam.

The Thames Barrier in London, England, is the largest flood barrier (with movable gates) in the world.

Flood barriers

Movable flood barriers have gates that can be closed to stop river waters from flooding certain areas, such as towns and cities, at high tide.

Hydroelectric power

Many dams are used to generate electrical power. In some countries, nearly all electrical energy is supplied in this way.

The dam contains large motors called turbines. Huge amounts of water are released through the barrier, into the river below, making the turbines spin. The spinning turbines drive generators to produce electrical power.

37

Flooded

Whether it is due to a sudden downpour of heavy rainfall or a long period of very wet weather, too much rain can cause rivers to flood. Flooding can cause serious problems for people, animals, and the land nearby.

Here comes the rain...

In periods of heavy rainfall, the ground gets completely soaked with water. This forces lots of rainfall to flow overground – directly into rivers and streams, which may then overflow.

A flash flood

Some floods happen without warning, often after a thunderstorm. In steep, narrow valleys and gorges there is nowhere for the water to go, so it gushes downhill – very quickly.

Evacuation

Sometimes, cities, towns, and villages are so badly hit by flooding that people have to be evacuated (taken away) from the area. The risk of landslides, drowning, and illness means that it is simply too dangerous to stay there. Trained rescue workers help people to get away safely.

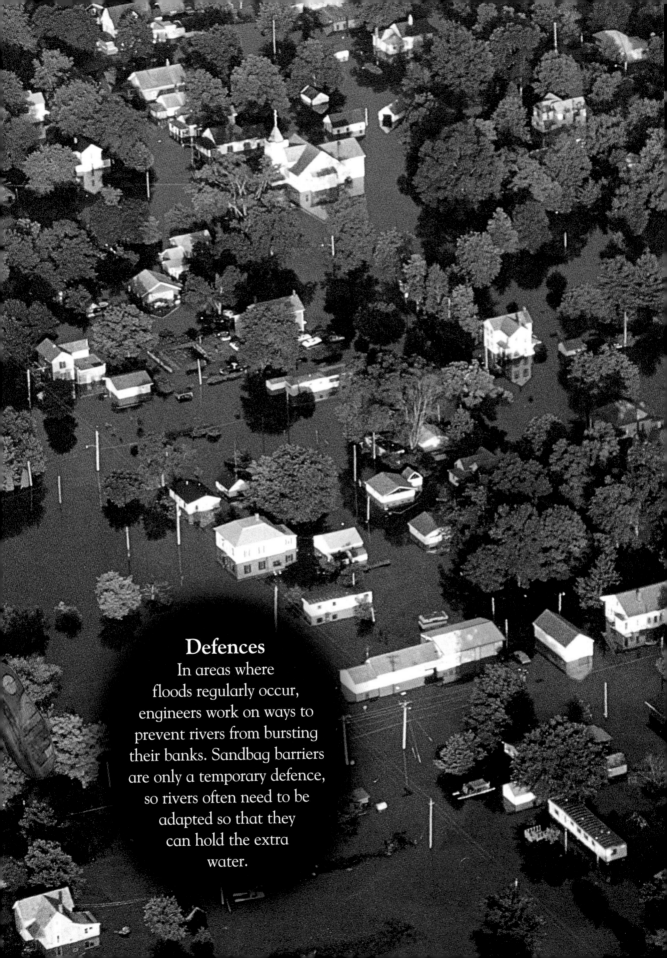

Defences
In areas where
floods regularly occur,
engineers work on ways to
prevent rivers from bursting
their banks. Sandbag barriers
are only a temporary defence,
so rivers often need to be
adapted so that they
can hold the extra
water.

Dried out

A long period of dry weather, with much less rainfall than usual for the time of year (or none at all), is called a drought. During a drought, rivers, streams, lakes, and ponds carry much less water – and they can even dry up completely.

Where the water goes...

The water in rivers and lakes gets heated up by the Sun, and rises up into the atmosphere as water vapour. This is called evaporation. When there is not enough rainfall to replace this lost water, rivers and lakes can dry out very easily.

A dried-out lake in Thailand (above)

Farmers in hot climates often rely on regular floods to bring water and nutrients to the soil, which will boost plant growth.

Periods of little rainfall mean that aquifers may not refill, causing village wells to dry up.

How wells work
Wells, dug into the earth, get their water from underground rock clusters called "aquifers", which store rainwater that has soaked deep into the ground.

Trapped
It looks as if somebody has carved an intricate pattern into the mud at the bottom of this drying lake in Tanzania. These shapes are in fact caused by the bodies of catfish that have become trapped by the shortage of water.

Crop damage
All plants need water to make their own food for growth and survival, so drought is bad news for farmers. Their communities depend on healthy crops.

41

Polluted

Imagine living somewhere that is always dirty. Sadly, this is the case for some wildlife as a result of pollution in rivers and lakes. River clean-up projects around the world are helping to improve this situation.

Polluted waste water is being pumped out of a mine through this pipe – poisoning a freshwater river.

Waste-coloured waters

Rivers are often polluted by liquid waste products from factories, or pest control treatments used on farms. Very strict laws have been created to try and make sure that industries deal with their waste properly.

Hard to breathe

Waste from boats and industries located in river estuaries can have a serious effect on wildlife. Oil can spill from boat engines or tankers, and this blocks the supply of oxygen to fish.

Factories are often built close to rivers, which can be used as a water supply.

"Lime drops"

In Scandinavia, many lakes are very clear – but this is actually the result of acid rain pollution, which reduces the amount of life in the lakes. This helicopter is dropping lime into a lake, to cancel out the life-killing acid.

Going with the flow

This lady in Nepal is washing her dishes in river water, but this may not be entirely safe. Upstream, the river is polluted. The dirty water can flow a long way, affecting both people and animals further downstream.

Out of the ordinary

They may just be pits in the ground full of water, or snaking, watery chutes on their way to the sea – but lakes and rivers can be highly impressive in their size, appearance, and what they contain.

The amazing Amazon

The mighty Amazon River, in South America, carries more water than any other river in the world – enough flow to fill one million bathtubs in less than a minute.

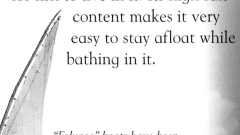

Dead salty

Not all lakes are fresh water filled. There is a lake between Israel and Jordan named the "Dead Sea", because it contains too much salt for fish to live in it. Its high salt content makes it very easy to stay afloat while bathing in it.

"Felucca" boats have been around for centuries, and are still the main form of transport on the Nile today.

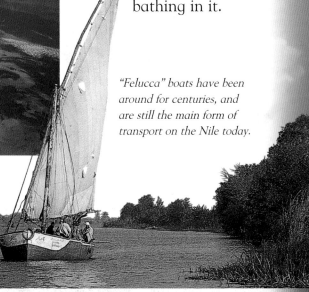

The never-ending Nile

The River Nile is made up of two rivers, the White Nile and the (smaller) Blue Nile, which combine to form the longest river on the planet. It measures 6,648 km (4,132 miles) long from source to sea.

The Mastigias jellies in Jellyfish Lake contain special cells that allow them to produce their own food simply by basking in sunlight.

ellyfish Lake

Millions of years ago, changes in the land created a lake – in Palau, Micronesia – that is now completely cut off from the sea. The lake still contains a variety of ellyfish that once only ved in the ocean.

Divers can swim among the stingless jellies of Jellyfish Lake in total safety.

Water thoughts

● Over time, the *Mastigias* ellyfish in Jellyfish Lake have lost their ability to ting, while the same pecies in the nearby ocean an still inflict a nasty bite.

● The Amazon River collects vater from a region more than 0 times the size of France.

Glossary

This A-Z glossary explains important words to do with rivers and lakes.

Acid rain water in rain, hail, or snow that is polluted as a result of certain chemicals and waste products being released into the atmosphere.

Aquifer a rock formation, underground, that is capable of holding large amounts of water. Aquifers provide water for wells.

Atmosphere the layer of gases that make up air around the Earth. The air includes the gases that plants and animals need to breathe.

Bayou a boggy, marshy area beside a lake or river.

Billabong this word, mainly used in Australia, is another name for an ox-bow lake.

Buoyancy the ability of some objects and living creatures – such as aquatic birds – to float on the surface of water.

Camouflage the way animals hide themselves by blending in with their natural surroundings – often using the shape and colour of their body parts.

Cascade a small waterfall. A gentle flow of water dropping down over rocky steps of land.

Cataract a waterfall, bigger than a cascade, where a large amount of water gushes over a rocky drop.

Climate the climate of a certain region describes the type of weather it usually has over one whole year. For example, a

"mountain" climate usually has a great deal of snow, rain, and cold weather for much of the year.

Crater a bowl-like hollow, or depression, that has formed in the landscape – for example, at the top of an inactive volcano. Over time, "crater lakes" can form as water gradually fills these hollows

Current a "path" of water, within a river or lake, that flows in a certain direction.

Dam a bank, wall, or barrier built to block the flow of water in a stream or river.

Discharge the measurement of the size and speed of a river's flow

Drought a long period of dry weather, during which an area receives much less rainfall than usual for the time of year.

Erosion when rock or soil is loosened and carried off by glaciers, rivers, winds, and waves.

Estuary the wide mouth of a river, where its fresh water meets the salty tidal waters of the sea.

Evaporation the process through which liquid water heats up and changes into water vapour (a gas, which rises into the atmosphere.

Fertilization the step in the reproduction of living things that takes place when cells from a male and female combine – for example, when a sperm fertilizes an egg.

Fresh water the water from rain

hail, and snow, which flows in streams and rivers, that is not salty.

Gills the special organs that aquatic (water-dwelling) creatures, such as fish, use for breathing (taking in oxygen) underwater.

Glacier a huge collection of ice, added to by snow in mountainous areas. Glaciers slowly creep downhill, where they either melt or break up into icebergs.

Gorge a deep, narrow, steep-sided area of land through which rivers usually flow.

Ice caps the permanent coverings of ice found in the Earth's polar regions and on mountain-tops in cold climates.

Irrigation the adding of extra water to plants and farmland, often using fresh water from rivers and reservoirs.

Larva an early stage in the life of some animals, after birth or hatching, when the young animal looks very different to a fully-developed adult.

Loch this Scottish word is another name for a lake, or a large area of seawater enclosed by land (but not on all sides).

Meander the name for a gentle curve or sharp bend in the course of a river (in its middle stages).

Migration the name for the way animals travel long distances to a new home at certain times of the year, or at certain stages of their life – often in large groups.

Ox-bow lake a "cut-off loop" of water, formed when a river meander gets so big – and the water wears away at the land so much – that it becomes a separate lake beside the main river course.

Oxygen a gas contained in the atmosphere that is breathed in, or absorbed, by almost all living creatures to release energy from food.

Pollution damage to the environment caused by chemical dumping or dirty waste products.

Precipitation the general name for the fresh water that falls from clouds as rain, hail, or snow.

Predator an animal that hunts and eats other animals (its prey).

Prey an animal that is hunted and eaten by other animals (its predators).

Reservoir an artificial (man-made) lake used to store water for purposes such as irrigation.

Salt water the water in the seas and oceans, which has salt and other minerals dissolved into it. The salt and minerals mainly wash into the sea from the land.

Sediment small pieces of solid material that get dragged along with the flow of the river water, and then settle to the river bed when the flow slows down.

Spawning the process by which certain animals produce a mass of eggs, and lay them in water, to breed (have babies).

Tadpole the name for the larva (young stage) of a frog or toad.

Tributary a stream that runs into another to form a larger stream with a greater discharge.

Valley a lowland area between hills or mountains. Rivers flow through valleys, and are fed by the precipitation that moves down from the higher ground.

Water cycle the process during which water heats up, rises into the atmosphere, forms clouds, falls as precipitation, and then returns to the ocean via rivers.

Water vapour water in the form of a gas, after it has evaporated.

White-water rapids the fast-flowing part of a river that flows through steep, rocky land, causing the water to foam. This foaming makes the water appear white.

Index

Crested newt tadpole

Acknowledgements

Dorling Kindersley would like to thank the following people for their help in making this book: Venice Shone for original artwork illustrations; Sarah Mills and Gemma Woodward for DK Picture Library research; Abbie Collinson and Sonia Whillock for design assistance.

Picture credits

The publisher would like to thank the following for their kind permission to reproduce their photographs:
a=above; c=centre; b=below; l=left; r=right; t=top

Bruce Coleman Ltd.: Erwin & Peggy Bauer 13cl; Jane Burton 16clb, 28bc; Jules Cowan 5br; Gerald S. Cubitt 4-5; Paolo Fioratti 1; Jeff Foott 34c, 34clb, 34cb; Sven Halling 22-23b; Joe McDonald 30cl; Dr. Eckart Pott 35b; Marie Read 27b; Hans Reinhard 22c; Tom Schandy 33tr, 47tr; Kim Taylor 17c, 48c. Corbis: Yann Arthus-Bertrand 32; Richard Gross 37br; James Marshall 14tl; Buddy Mays 36; Stephanie Maze 43tc; David Muench 9br; Jeffrey L. Rotman 45; Sygma/Allen Martin 38cl; Patrick Ward 14cr. Joe Cornish: 15. Getty Images: Cousteau Society 8br; Pascal Crapet 8cra; Cameron Davidson 20ac; Terry Donnelly 21cl; Howie Garber 6l; Chris Noble 8l; Richard Passmore 44tr; Manoj Shah 22cb; Grant Symon 4tl, 4cla, 4tll;

Robert Van Der Hilst 9. ImageState: AGE Fotostock 37tr; Alan Blair 6r. Katz Pictures: FSP/Gamma 39, 40-41b. FLPA – Images of Nature: E. & D. Hosking 14bl. NASA: 44bl. Natural History Museum: 23r. N.H.P.A.: Daniel Heuclin 31br; Dave Watts 10cra; David Woodfall 7r; GI Bernard 17br; Kevin Schafer 26c; Lutra 11c; Stephen Dalton 16cr, 22cb; T. Kitchin & V. Hurst 35t; Tom and Therisa Stack 23cl. Oxford Scientific Films: 17br, 28c; Paulo De Oliveira 2l, 3r, 48l, 48r; Professor Jack Dermid 17tr, 29cla; Max Gibbs 2bc, 3cb, 3br; Joan/Root/SAL 41tl; Chris Knights/SAL 33cla; Victoria McCormick/ AA 34bc; John Mitchell 16br; Michael Pitts 21tc; Edward Parker 27tl; Andrew Plumptre 22tr; F. Polking/ OKAPIA 16tl; Herb Segars/AA 23; Tom Ulrich 13tr. Pa Photos: EPA 38br. Science Photo Library: Worldsat International 23tl; Still Pictures: 40tr; Andre Bartschi 44cl; Gilles Corniere 42tr; Glen Christian 41tr; Mark Edwards 43cra; Reinhard Janke 42cl; Yves Lefevre 31; Max Milligan 7l; Tim Rice 33cr, 46l, 47r; Hartmut Schwarzbach 42-43b. Warren Photographic: 20-21. Jerry Young: 21b.

Jacket credits – Bruce Coleman Ltd.: Jane Burton front br; Dr. Eckart Pott front bl. Getty Images: Doug Armand front bc; Cameron Davidson front t; Rick Rusing back.

All other images © Dorling Kindersley. For further information see: www.dkimages.com